INTEGRITY AT WORK:

A PERSONAL APPROACH
TO ETHICAL DECISION MAKING

BROTHER HERMAN ZACCARELLI, C.S.C.

iUniverse, Inc.
New York   Bloomington

Integrity At Work:
A Personal Approach to Ethical Decision Making.

iUniverse books may be ordered through booksellers or by contacting:

iUniverse
1663 Liberty Drive
Bloomington, IN 47403
www.iuniverse.com
1-800-Authors (1-800-288-4677)

ISBN: 978-1-4401-8196-2 (sc)
ISBN: 978-1-4401-8197-9 (ebk)

Printed in the United States of America

iUniverse rev. date: 11/17/2009

DEDICATION

Integrity At Work: A Personal Approach To Ethical Decision Making is dedicated to three individuals who have accompanied me for over thirty years in my professional life.

For their friendship, as well as their tireless assistance to me on myriad projects, I dedicate this book to:

> Donald Christie, President
> American Tax and Business Shoppe
> Winter Park, Florida
>
> Russell Pottle, President
> Tennessee Bookman
> Fairview, Tennessee
>
> Cameron W. Watson, President
> Fluid Graphics Corporation
> Alpharetta, Georgia

TABLE OF CONTENTS

Section 4. Integrity in External Work Relationships

Section 5: Measuring Ethical Success

FOREWORD

I have known Brother Herman for over thirty years and have treasured his friendship and teachings over this time. I have encouraged him in the writing of this book; to share his knowledge of ethics which is so important every day in our lives.

I am in the business of buying and selling companies. Critical to this process is learning whether the leadership on the other side is honorable and has integrity.

Very basic and not even in the formal program, one assumes automatically that you are dealing with people of integrity. This can be a very expensive error and result in the loss of considerable treasure and reputation.

Simply put, you must ask yourself:

- Is the leader on the other side a person of integrity?
- Does the leader tell the truth?
- Does the management team provide complete and accurate data?
- Will they perform as promised?

The determination of these qualities bound up in the concept of integrity does not come about automatically. The skill must be learned and that is what this book is about. When you are finished with this work you should have a sense of the place and importance of integrity in your business and personal life.

Integrity At Work: A Personal Approach To Ethical Decision Making will help its readers learn more about integrity and its many definitions. Use it as your guide and compass in all of your dealings for success.

George C. St. Laurent, Jr.

ACKNOWLEDGEMENTS

For the many hours devoted to this project I would like to thank David K. Hayes, Ph.D. and his excellent editorial team at Panda Professionals (www.pandapros.com).

Dr. Hayes's group has edited and in myriad other ways assisted in the development and publication of a number of my books and projects. I am proud to say that David is a consummate professional. At its best, professional writing makes clear thoughts possible, accessible, reader-friendly and memorable. Experienced authors know that a successful publication such as this one engages the wisdom, skills, and background of individual minds beyond that of the writer alone. I am indebted to Dr. Hayes' team for adding their considerable breadth of knowledge and for his personally giving the manuscript expert scrutiny for both content and quality. I would also like to recognize the staff at IUniverse Publishing for their hard work in helping to produce this volume.

As always, the priests and brothers of the Congregation of Holy Cross have supported me in every endeavor in the service of professional education and for that support I am exceedingly appreciative.

I am especially grateful for George C. St. Laurent, Jr.; St. Laurent Properties of Vancouver, Washington for agreeing to write the forward for this book as well as for his immense personal support of the overall project.

Finally, and perhaps most importantly, I would like to acknowledge the many food service professionals (from entry-level workers to those in management) that I have met and learned so much from over the years. I am convinced that what one becomes in life is shaped chiefly by all of the experiences and all the thoughts you've ever had; and by all of the people who have touched your life; no matter how briefly. For the many foodservice professionals I have met I will be eternally indebted as they are the ones who touched me and, in doing so, inspired me to conceive and bring *Integrity At Work: A Personal Approach To Ethical Decision Making* to fruition.

Brother Herman Zaccarelli C.S.C.

SECTION 1

Workplace Ethics

Topic 1: What Are Ethics?

Consider This

The average person makes thousands of decisions every day. Most of them are easy. Decisions like what time to get up, what to have for breakfast, and when to go to work. These decisions mean you do something as a result. Your decisions lead to actions.

You decide to get up at 7 a.m., so you get out of bed at that time. You decide to have eggs and toast for breakfast, so you make them. You need to arrive at work by 8:00 a.m., so you leave your home in time to get there before 8:00. Sometimes the actions you take as a result of a decision are pretty easy to perform.

Ethics are behavior based upon your view of what is right or wrong. Ethical decisions can be hard to make. This is because most often the actions that follow these decisions directly impact others as well as yourself. Often, these decisions are not easily reached.

Your own views of the right, wrong, good, or bad things to do are shaped by your personal life experience. As a result, your ethical views can be influenced by others, but they come from inside you. Your own ethics will likely be similar to many others you meet; but are likely to be very different from some people you encounter.

This book will lead you on a journey of discovering your own view on ethics. In turn you will be perfectly positioned to create a personal code of ethics that will enhance your decision making and your life.

> *"What lies behind us and what lies before us are tiny matters compared to what lies within us."*
> *Ralph Waldo Emerson*

Put It To Work

All work requires interaction with others. You may be an entrepreneur, a CEO, a manager or a supervisor. You may interact with co-workers, employees, customers or suppliers. The one thing that is certain is that if you are employed in today's workforce, the diversity of individuals you will meet is greater than at any time in the past.

That means diversity of race, age, nationality, religion, gender, sexual orientation, and even ethics. In fact, many of the same characteristics that make people different also make their views of right and wrong behavior different.

And that means you are likely to encounter individuals whose opinions about right and wrong behavior are quite different from your own. One challenge you will face at work is how to hold firm to your own ethical views while at the same time acknowledging and respecting those individuals who hold ethical views that may be very different from yours.

What Do You Think?

1. Do you think the diversity of individuals you encounter at your own work is increasing or decreasing? _____
   _____

2. Have you found that your opinion of behavior that is appropriate or not appropriate at work differs from your co workers? _____

3. Do you think it is important to maintain your own sense of right and wrong behavior even when others disagree with you?
   _____

   Why? _____

Take It Away

"Your personal ethics reflect who you are, but more importantly, they suggest who you will become."

SECTION 1

Workplace Ethics

Topic 2: Ethics and Morality

Consider This

Close your eyes a moment and image your best possible Saturday. In your vision did you wake up at 6:00 a.m. ready to have your first cup of coffee and perhaps a morning jog followed by lively conversation with one of your closest friends? If so, you are clearly a morning person. If, however, the idea of immediate action, let alone social interaction, prior to 10:00 a.m. on your dream Saturday makes you groan and want to pull the covers back over your head, you are likely an evening person.

Morning people love their unique view of the world and they love other morning people. Evening people mesh well with other evening people. But neither group truly thrives in the company of the other.

People with a specific set of ethical views often seek out others who share those same views. Ethical views about proper behavior that are shared among a group are called *morals*. The group may also share a common religion, profession or cultural background. In fact, membership in the group may be dependent upon accepting the group's moral views. The good news is that close interaction with others who share values can be empowering and even very comforting for you.

The danger with groups, however, is that they are not infallible. Even worse, their subtle or not so subtle pressure to conform to all of their moral views can make you believe you should replace your own ethical judgments with theirs. When that happens, a group membership that was meant to be empowering can become overpowering. Group morality and group membership makes sense only when they validate, not dictate, your own ethical judgments.

> *"Those who stand for nothing fall for anything."*
> *Alexander Hamilton*

Put It To Work

Some work groups are famous for their shared ethical views. Newspaper reporters, for example, are virtually united in their belief that it is unethical to reveal their confidential news sources. The moral code of doctors, lawyers and ministers includes the prohibition of sharing confidential patient, client or church member information with others.

In these examples, it would not be surprising to find that any group member who rejected the majority shared view of proper behavior would be considered unethical, and would likely subject themselves to a negative response from their work group.

In most cases, when a work group member's morale compass is consistent with the one encountered in the workplace, ethics-related conflicts are minimized. This is one reason why it can be so tempting to simply replace your own view of ethical behavior with that of your work group or business organization.

Morals are ethical values shared by a group and *morality* is the way the group views each member's adherence to the group values. It is important to remember, however, that traveling a well-beaten path doesn't mean you are going the right way. History shows that group morality does not reflect ethical behavior 100% of the time.

Because that is true, you need to retain and follow your own moral compass; even when it means resisting the pressure exerted by a group trying to advance its own moral positions. In nearly every case, if you do not stay true to your own convictions, you will soon find that everyone in your group, *except you*, really admires you!

What Do You Think?

1. Have you ever found yourself in a work situation in which your ethical values were in conflict with those of your peers?

   _____

   What did you do? _____

2. Do you think subtle group pressure can cause ethical persons to condone or engage in behaviors they feel are unethical? _____

3. What would you advise a friend to do if "getting along" at his or her workplace meant "going along" with actions that a friend strongly believed were the wrong thing for him or her to do? _____

Take It Away

> "The higher the price of nonconformity,
> the higher the value of your independence."

SECTION 1

Workplace Ethics

Topic 3: Ethics and the Law

Consider This

Each year almost nine million dogs and cats are euthanized in the U.S. because there are not enough homes or resources to keep them in shelters. In California alone, 750,000 to 1 million animals each year are killed for this reason. Nationally, more than 60% of the animals brought to animal shelters die there. In the U.S. there is no law requiring pet owners to neuter their dogs or cats.

Some observers believe it is ethically and morally wrong to allow domesticated animals to breed excessively. When enough people ultimately share this moral value it is likely a law will be passed that addresses this unfortunate issue.

Laws are rules of conduct that are considered so important they are enforced by a society. Laws can be considered mandatory rules of conduct. Violating a law typically leads to some type of societal punishment.

The history of humankind records ever changing laws seeking to mandate behavior that reflects the society's shared ethical beliefs. Laws change. Right and wrong behavior is unchanging. Society's view of what is right or wrong is typically altered only after awareness of an unethical action's impact on others is fully recognized.

The standards of what constitutes justifiable behavior come first. Laws follow after a society recognizes the truth behind the ethical behavior.

While laws can enforce ethical actions, they do not create the need for them. It should never be the case that people behave ethically simply because laws force them to do so.

> *"Good people do not need laws to tell them to act responsibly, while bad people will seek a way around the laws."*
> *Plato*

Put It To Work

Managers who define ethical behavior based only on its legality face a variety of challenges. One challenge is that laws are not equally applied in all settings.

For example, assume you own a business and decide to place a very large and very profitable order with one of your suppliers. If that supplier decides to thank you for your order by sending a case of fine champagne to your home, you could legally accept it. If, however, you worked for a state government, the Federal government or any number of other business entities, accepting an identical gift could make you guilty of accepting a kickback and subject you to loss of your job or even criminal charges!

Buyers with professional ethics do not accept kickbacks or bribes, even when doing so is legal.

An even greater challenge for managers seeking to define their behavior based on its legality is the fact that laws change as society perfects its view of right behavior. There are numerous examples of this in business including how employees are to be hired as well as how employees are to be treated while at work.

Prior to passage of the Civil Rights Act of 1964, employers in the U.S. could legally reject a job applicant based solely on the applicant's race or religion. Ethical managers know that *prior* to 1964, discrimination based on race or religion was wrong even though it was legal.

Ethical managers do stay current with laws affecting their businesses, but they do not base their ethical decisions solely on what they are permitted to do. Instead, they base their decisions on what they know is the right thing to do.

What Do You Think?

1. Have you ever been treated in an unethical way by a business or individual? _____ Were their actions legal? _____
   _____

2. In your own profession, is there any act that is legal but that you would still consider to be unethical? _____ Why do you consider that action to be wrong? _____
   _____

3. How would you react to a colleague who defended his or her unethical action by saying the actions were okay because they were not illegal? _____
   _____

Take It Away

"*Law and justice are not incompatible;*
despite a good number of appearances to the contrary."

SECTION 1

Workplace Ethics

Topic 4: The Myth of Business Ethics

Consider This

If you have ever been lucky enough to watch the sunset over an ocean, you know you saw a literal spectrum of color change. The water slowly turns from turquoise green to shimmering silver as the sun moves from placid yellow to a fiery red. The sky's bright blue turns to midnight blue as the clouds transform from white to pinks, oranges, yellows and golds.

To the non-artist, it might seem that painting such a scene would require an almost infinite number of different colors. Talented painters capturing that beautiful sunset, however, know they need only to skillfully blend the artist's three primary colors of red, blue and yellow to portray the scene's splendor.

As with the many colors in a sunset, some view ethics when applied to a business setting as multifaceted and highly complex. They should not.

Just as painters astutely blend their three-color palate to capture nuances of light, managers blend their ethics, morals and the law when determining ethical behavior in a variety of business settings.

It is important to recognize that there are no unique ethics to be utilized only when working. An individual's ethics, morals and laws are not different when they are at home, at school, at church or even in their personal relationships. Rather, an individual's same fundamental ethics, morals and the law when combined in an appropriate way should form the basis for right behavior in every setting.

> *"Relativity applies to physics, not ethics."*
> *Albert Einstein*

Put It To Work

Some managers feel that the ethics they apply at work must be different from those they use outside of work because the main purpose of a business is to maximize financial returns to its owners or stockholders. Under this view, any legal (or even lightly punished!) activity that increases profitability is automatically legitimate. These managers take the position that at work; if an action is legal to do, then it is O.K. to do.

But ethical managers know that a business has moral duties that reach well beyond serving the interests of its owners or stockholders. These moral responsibilities extend to all those who have an interest in the conduct of the business including employees, customers, vendors, the local community, or even society as a whole. For these mangers, the same ethics that guide their interpersonal behavior and the morals that govern their group action are equally as important as following the law.

The intermingling of ethics, morals and legal duties can certainly vary based on where you work. In a highly regulated industry, knowledge of laws may be extremely important. In many non-profit and other business organizations mutual moral values and a shared view of justice may take precedence. In very small organizations, interpersonal ethics are most often of greatest importance.

Artists carefully blend only a few primary colors to capture their complex vision of the world. In the same way, the thoughtful merging of your personal ethics, morals and respect for law permits you to create your own unique and very personal set of business ethics.

What Do You Think?

1. Do you think the ethics you use at work can be very different from those you use away from work? _____
    _____

2. Can you think of an action that would be legal and increase profits but still be the wrong thing for a business to do? _____ Why do you consider that action to be wrong?
    _____

3. How would you respond to colleagues who state that being unethical at work is O.K. if it helps the business increase its profits? _____
    _____

Take It Away

> *"The first measure of a business's success is its ability to make profits in an honorable way."*

SECTION 1

Workplace Ethics

Topic 5: Workplace Integrity: How Ethics Pay Off

Consider This

If you are a Secret Service agent guarding the President of the United States, your job is to ensure the safety of the person who could arguably be considered the single most powerful person on earth. It's a very important job.

As a part of the department of Homeland Security, the Secret Service agents selected to serve as Presidential bodyguards are members of a very exclusive group. Well-educated and highly trained, their job descriptions include the one task that separates them from every other federal agent. If called upon, their *job* is to step in front of a bullet intended for the President!

Certainly, no one takes such a job for the pay!

Interestingly, it is at the very time their personal risk is at its highest level that they must demonstrate their ability to overcome their natural fear and do what they have pledged to do. At that critical moment, the agent's commitment to purpose, loyalty to country and to their own honor will override concerns about their personal safety.

Some critics believe far too many Americans put their own self interests above all others. It may be true of some Americans, but they certainly can't say that about everyone.

> *"A heart needs only its own voice to do what is right."*
> *Vanna Bonta*

Put It To Work

Ethics are behavior based on your opinions about right and wrong. Integrity is how steadfast you are in maintaining those ethical views. In a business setting it may seem like it would be easy to maintain your integrity. Often it is not.

That's because in many cases there is a real cost associated with strongly preserving your view of right and wrong behavior. In the short run, the cost of maintaining your integrity can seem very high. Sales may be lower. Profits may be reduced. You may not be given the promotion.

What you will get to keep, however, is your integrity. Integrity is a one-of-a-kind reward because only you can give it to yourself. And only you can give it up. It can't be taken away from you.

Those who count on you to display your integrity certainly expect you will when the cost of doing so is low. That's the easy part.

Your co-workers, your family, your community, and most importantly you, learn most about your integrity when you face the bullets at work. It is in those trying times you can display the self-respect, honesty, dependability and tenaciousness that define your own character.

What Do You Think?

1. Have you ever paid a price for being ethical at work? _____
_____

2. Have you ever seen someone at work abandon their professed values when it makes things easier for them? _____
_____

3. Who in your own life counts on you to display your integrity in challenging times? _____
_____

Take It Away

> *"Integrity is the measure of faith you put in yourself."*

SECTION 2

Self-Examination for the Ethical Manager

Topic 1: The Need for Self-Examination

Consider This

In the days before electronic navigational instruments, sailors faced tremendous risks when they travelled at sea. In addition to storms and hidden reefs, they faced the very real prospect of getting hopelessly lost and then running out of food or fresh water.

When they were close to the shore, they could use known *landmarks* like buildings, rivers or mountains to tell them where they were. But in the middle of the ocean, there are no landmarks so the potential to become lost grew significantly.

Fortunately, there were things that sailors could see wherever they sailed. The sun, moon and stars would always be visible regardless of a sailor's location. For those who knew how to read them, these *skymarks* were extremely helpful. For example, because the North Star always points northward, steering the boat toward that specific star always resulted in a northerly path. But simply knowing there was a North Star was not enough. The sailors had to *use* it as a guide to get the right direction.

Skymarks like the sun, moon and stars helped sailors understand where they were. Just as importantly, by assessing their position, they could best chart a course for where they wanted to go. Of course, the sailors could not simply evaluate their location one time and be finished for their entire voyage. Navigational assessments had to be on-going and continual. Only by this careful examination and re-examination of their present position could they chart the future course needed to arrive safely at their intended destination.

> *"The unexamined life is not worth living."*
> Socrates

Put It To Work

If you are a manager you will undoubtedly face ethical challenges in your future. Such challenges are unavoidable. When they do occur, you will need a method for assessing what you should do about them.

Some managers believe that if they are cautious enough they will never face ethical dilemmas. Not true. Indeed, it may be true that if early sailors never left the coasts they would never have faced navigational challenges.

It would also be true, however, that those same sailors would never have made great discoveries about their world or about themselves.

Today, effective managers simply cannot allow themselves to coast. Staying on a steady course requires that you too develop navigational tools for assessing where you are and where you want to go in your role as an ethical manager.

Not everyone will agree about what is ethical at all times and in all circumstances. You are able to stay on a steady course when you have a systematic way to examine and work through an ethical challenge or dilemma. A proper course of action can only be arrived at through an honest self-examination and application of your own ethical viewpoints when the need arises.

What Do You Think?

1. Have you ever experienced an ethical dilemma at work? _____
   _____

2. Who do you think is responsible for the ethical decisions you make when you are at work? _____

3. In your experience does thinking about the possible consequences of your actions usually help you make better decisions about what to do in difficult situations? _____ Why? _____

Take It Away

"Your personal decisions chart your professional course."

SECTION 2

Self-Examination for the Ethical Manager

Topic 2: The Self-Examination Process: Applying 3-Key Questions

Consider This

In 2007, there were over 800 million passenger cars and trucks operating across the globe. That number is estimated to exceed one billion by 2010. Millions of new and used cars and trucks are sold each year.

Shopping for a new vehicle is an exciting process, but with literally millions to choose from, it can be daunting. Most buyers make the process much easier by consciously (or subconsciously) posing a series of questions to themselves. The answer to each question helps guide their buying behavior.

For example, a buyer may first ask *"Do I want to buy a car or a truck?* If the answer is a *car*, then all trucks can be eliminated from the selection process.

Next, the buyer establishes a price range. They may ask *"How much do I want to spend?* All vehicles priced outside the range indicated by their answer can be eliminated.

As the questioning continues, buyers may ask themselves questions about desired color, style, mileage, dependability or any other factor of importance to them. Each question is designed to improve the choice made.

When the time comes, asking and answering the right questions will help you buy the car that is right for you and not merely a car someone else wants to sell you.

Questions and answers about alternative choices are important because in car buying, as with life, you can never escape the consequences of your own decisions!

> *"It is our choices that show what we truly are, far more than our abilities."*
> Joanne Kathleen (JK) Rowling

Put It To Work

When you need to make an important decision it helps to have a plan of action to guide you. As a manager, you will face ethical dilemmas and when you do, a step-by-step action plan can help you choose the right thing to do.

The answers you give to three important YES or NO questions can help you determine whether an action you are considering is ethical or not ethical. The actual form of the question will vary somewhat based on the specific ethical situation faced, but ultimately the questions are:

> Would I tell others what I did?
>
> Would I care if it happened to me?
>
> What if everyone did it?

In the remainder of this book you will learn why the answers to these key self-examination questions are so important and how to use the questions to make ethical decisions.

An answer of NO to the first question means you likely feel the action under consideration is wrong and you should not do it. An answer of YES to the first question does *not* mean you consider that proposed action ethical. A YES answer does, however, mean that you should ask yourself the second question.

An answer of NO to the second question means you feel the act is wrong and you should not do it. Again, an answer of YES to the question does *not* mean you consider that the proposed action is ethical. A YES answer does, however, mean that you should ask yourself the final question.

Like the first two questions, an answer of NO to this question means you believe the action under consideration is likely unethical. You should not do it. An answer of YES to this question and the previous questions means you believe the action is ethical and you would comfortable doing it.

In every case; you decide. That's good because only you can be held responsible for the decisions you make and the ethical actions you take!

What Do You Think?

1. Have you ever decided *not* to do something because you secretly feared others might find out that you did it? _____

   _____

2. For most people, the Golden Rule (*Do unto others as you would have others do unto you!*) is a powerful deterrent to unethical behavior. Why do you think that is true? _____

   _____

3. Littering is a good example of an action that would not be very harmful if done by only one person; but devastating if done regularly by each of the nearly seven billion people on our planet. Can you think of other examples? _____

   _____

Take It Away

"*When you control your choices you control your future.*"

SECTION 2

Self-Examination for the Ethical Manager

Topic 3: Integrity Question #1: Would I Tell Others What I Did?

Consider This

In the diet industry business improves significantly every spring. Conventional wisdom is that the approaching summer makes people realize their wardrobes will soon consist of the shorts, T-shirts and swimwear popular in warm weather. Add to that realization a quick glance in the mirror and, in many cases, there is a renewed commitment to toning up, slimming down and looking good!

That's because people know that the summer means publicly exposing more of their physical appearance. And they naturally want to look their best. It would be a mistake, however, for observers to regard this annual interest in appearance improvement as a vain desire to please others. It is not.

In many areas of life people are more conscientious about themselves when they know others will be watching. But not because we let others dictate our standards. Rather, it demonstrates how we set our own standards and that we care how our standards are viewed by others.

When we must expose ourselves to others we display our personal standards publicly. We can't hide who we really are because others can see us clearly. When you see yourself in the mirror, you see what others will see. What will be visible to them is what you are proud to show. It is how you, not the crowds, view your reflection in the mirror that most defines you who are and who you will become.

> *"Tell me who admires you and loves you*
> *and I will tell you who you are."*
> *Charles Augustin Sainte-Beuve*

Put It To Work

In Hollywood it has often been said that all publicity (except an obituary!) is good publicity. That may be true for movie stars but business professionals know that widespread negative publicity that turns to public condemnation can quickly ruin a business or a career.

Perhaps that is one more good reason why it is so important to carefully consider how others will view the action you take in an ethically questionable situation.

It would not likely be hard for you to identify examples of entertainment figures, businesses, or even your own co-workers whose unethical actions ultimately earned them the public condemnation of their fans, customers, or colleagues. Thus there are actually two good reasons why *"Would I tell others what I did"* is such a critical question to ask when deciding whether an action is ethical or not.

The first reason relates to what the action says about how you view yourself (and thus how others will view you). The second recognizes the very real and potentially devastating repercussions that can follow the public unveiling of unethical behavior.

To easily answer this first and most important self-assessment question, pose it to yourself this way:

> *Would I want everyone to read about what I did on the front page of my local newspaper tomorrow morning?*

If the answer is *No!*…then don't do it!

What Do You Think?

1. Have you ever know or heard of anyone whose unethical behavior significantly damaged their career when it was uncovered? _____

2. In professional sports it is often said that a foul is not really a foul unless the referee sees it. Do you think that same view can be applied to ethical behavior at work? _____.
   Why? _____

3. Think back to when you were growing up. Did you ever decide *not* to do something your friends were doing because you feared you might get caught if you did it? _____
   Do you regret that decision now? _____

Take It Away

> *"Admiration is the simple recognition that we
> often see in ourselves what others see in us."*

SECTION 2

Self-Examination for the Ethical Manager

Topic 4: Integrity Question #2: Would I Care If It Happened to Me?

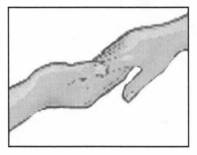

Consider This

On any given day, more than 700,000 people in the United States receive alcoholism treatment in either inpatient or outpatient settings. Variously referred to as anything from a genetic disease to a self-inflicted human frailty, most people know that alcoholics are those who persist in excessive consumption of alcohol despite the health problems and social consequences they ultimately experience.

What most people do not know is that Alcoholics Anonymous (AA), the international organization dedicated to helping individuals and families address alcohol addiction was started by Bill Wilson, a successful Wall Street executive whose career was ruined by excessive drinking.

In 1935 Wilson and Dr. Bob Smith organized what would become the world's largest international effort dedicated to helping the millions world-wide who suffer as the result of alcohol abuse. AA members are devoted to helping others address their alcoholism. And that's certainly a good thing.

But Wilson also strongly believed that by assisting other alcoholics, AA members would also be helping themselves. His experience indicated that those members who most actively reached out to assist others who were struggling would find their own struggles easier to bear.

Wilson found what many people who actively demonstrate their empathy for others come to know. Namely, that in many areas of life, the mere act of making things better for others makes things better for us as well.

> *"If you want others to be happy, practice compassion.*
> *If you want to be happy, practice compassion."*
> *Dalai Lama*

Put It To Work

There are really two reasons why *"Would I care if it happened to me?"* is such an insightful business inquiry when considering ethical behavior.

The first is that the best of business professionals truly care about the people affected by their actions. These professionals know that when you thoughtfully consider how you would feel if roles were reversed, it helps ensure you take the best interests of others into consideration before you act.

The second reason the question is important affects those who choose to ignore it. Those who pay no heed to how their acts would impact themselves or others ultimately find they are directly affected anyway.

This happens because ethical people seek to do business with others who are ethical. Think about it. If you know an organization or individual consistently treats their employees or customers unjustly you avoid it because you know they will treat you unfairly too.

The reverse is true. Unethical behavior draws to it those who admire its results. Unethical managers attract other workers and customers who are unethical. When they do, these unethical managers should not be surprised to find they themselves are treated poorly by others who also ignore the question *"Would I care if it happened to me?"* Not surprisingly, when unethical folks deal with other unethical folks, they do it unethically!

What Do You Think?

1. The *Golden Rule* has been identified by many as the most important rule to follow in any society. Why do you think that is so? _____

_____

2. Can you think of a time when you avoided a course of action because it would have negatively affected others? _____. What did you do instead? _____

_____

3. Do you know a person or company that you have stopped associating with because you do not trust them? _____

_____

Take It Away

"*Committing the Golden Rule to life, is the only reason for committing it to memory.*"

SECTION 2

Self-Examination for the Ethical Manager

Topic 5: Integrity Question #3: What If Everyone Did It?

Consider This

Usually when you consider the cumulative affects of a seemingly minor but undesirable behavior (like littering), it is pretty easy to imagine the devastating impact that would result if everyone, or even very large numbers of individuals, engaged in the activity. That's true, but the reverse is true as well.

In 1999, Dana Hork was a student at the University of Pennsylvania. Dana lived in Minnesota and as she prepared to move back there after her freshman year she realized she had accumulated a fair amount of loose change (pennies, nickels and dimes) that were too heavy to pack and take on the plane but too meaningful to leave behind.

Dana did some calculations and decided that by collecting even very small amounts of similar loose change from many students at many campuses across the US, a significant amount of money could be raised for charity.

Today **Change for Change**, the non-profit organization Dana founded in 1999, has multiple student chapters and has collected and disbursed hundreds of thousands of dollars. **Change for Change** is just one good example of the positive change that can occur when caring people inspire others to follow their lead. Even when the change they seek seems small at first!

> *"When your values are clear to you, making decisions becomes easier.*
> *Roy Disney*

Put It To Work

The "*What if everyone did it?*" question is an especially important one. If your answer to that question and the two previous questions indicate an action is O.K. for you, then you can be ethically comfortable doing it.

The importance of this question is easily illustrated by the employee who wonders if, while at work, spending five minutes per day twittering friends is ethical or not. After all, the amount of time involved is very small!

That same person might be interested to know that The Washington Post reported the results of a New York University professor's survey. The survey found that the Federal government directly and indirectly employees 14.6 million people. If each of those employees spent only five minutes per day twittering, the total lost productivity would be the same as if 150,000 Federal employees had called in sick to work that day!

The three-question action plan you have learned will be easy to remember if you practice using it. In the next sections of this book you will get a chance to do just that.

The ethical dilemmas presented are typical of the kinds you will encounter at work. They cannot always be avoided, but they can always serve to exhibit your character and demonstrate your integrity. When you use the three-question action plan, you will always be comfortable that you have made the best decision possible for you.

What Do You Think?

1. What is an activity that you know currently happens in your work place which could have an extremely negative effect if everyone there did it? _____

   _____

2. Ron is considering submitting for reimbursement some duplicate meal receipts acquired during a recent business trip. He is convinced he will not get caught doing it. Use the three question action plan to coach him on the ethics involved. Based on the results, should he do it? _____

3. Some professions, such as doctors or lawyers, have a formal code of ethics. Does your own profession have such a code? _____. Should it have one? _____

   _____

Take It Away

> *"Working with people who always do things right, never seems quite as satisfying as working with those who always do the right things."*

SECTION 3

Integrity in Internal Work Relationships

Topic 1: Ethical Situations with Your Supervisor

Consider This

During his lifetime, Jesse Owens was the world's fastest runner. Born a young black man in Alabama in 1913, Owens life story is fascinating. Overcoming the rampant racism that existed in the US at the time, he went on to represent the US in the 1936 Summer Olympics in Berlin, Germany. It was there that he achieved international fame by becoming the first American to win four Olympic gold medals in track and field.

In the years he trained for the Olympics, he was required to eat in black-only restaurants and sleep in black-only hotels. Despite these and other hardships unjustly placed upon him, Jesse Owens had talent and used it to achieve the kind of success other track and field athletes only dream about.

When he was asked about achieving dreams, he said "We all have dreams. But to make dreams come into reality, it takes an awful lot of determination, dedication, self-discipline and effort."

No one can guarantee success at work but it is true that achieving your greatest potential at work takes determination, dedication, self-discipline and effort even when things don't seem fair. It's those characteristics your boss hopes you display even when the circumstances surrounding your work appear to be unjust or unreasonable.

Like Jesse Owens, you can always choose to do the right things, regardless of the circumstances you face.

"Your real boss is the one who walks around under your hat."
Napoleon Hill

Put It To Work

"But Jonna, we need you on Saturday," said Mr. Larson, "we are going to be really busy all day."

"I understand that," replied Jonna "and I'm sorry but Saturday is the day my daughter graduates from college. I just can't miss that."

As a single mom, Jonna had, for more than ten years, saved and scrimped wherever she could to ensure her daughter Sylvia could finish college. Saturday was the long awaited day Sylvia would graduate, but Mr. Larson, her boss, was insisting she work that day.

"Jonna, if you don't come in on Saturday, everyone else in your department will have to work over-time. And they won't be happy about that, you can bet on it!" said Mr. Larson.

What Do You Think?

Assume you were Jonna and ask yourself these versions of the three key self-examination questions:

1. Would you care if the boss explained to your co-workers that the reason they were required to work extra was because you were going to the graduation? _____

2. If you were the person in charge, would you allow your employees to take off a scheduled work day if they had a similar personal reason? _____

3. How would you feel if everyone on your work team wanted your boss to change your own work schedule when they wanted time off? _____

Take It Away

"The best way to learn how to lead others with integrity is to practice on you every day."

SECTION 3

Integrity in Internal Work Relationships

Topic 2: Ethical Situations with your Co-Workers

Consider This

The University of San Francisco (USF) embodies the rich vision of St. Ignatius of Loyola, who founded the Society of Jesus (the Jesuits) in 1540. Jesuit education affirms the ultimate goodness of the world as created, loved, and redeemed by God; it seeks to find God in all things. And in 1951, USF fielded a football team (the Dons) that reflected ultimate goodness as well!

That year, the football team was undefeated, united and uninvited. It should have been asked to play in a bowl game to decide the national championship.

In the early part of the 1950s, however, many bowl games were given to teams with only white players, or teams that would at least not play their black players during the bowl game. When it was time to be invited to a bowl, the Dons were told they would have to leave their two black teammates at home.

In an unprecedented move, the team members refused to accept a bid that would not allow everyone to play. Nor did the university continue the football program, despite the fact that an unprecedented nine of that team's players would eventually play in the National Football League (NFL) and four would be inducted into the NFL Hall of Fame. Pete Rozelle, another team member, would serve for 30 years as commissioner of the NFL.

When people say that, on many levels, the best football *team* you never heard of is the 1951 University of San Francisco Dons team, it's really pretty hard to argue with them. On a real team, teammates count.

> *"Individual commitment to a group effort. That's what makes a team work, a company work, a society work, a civilization work."*
> *Vince Lombardi*

Put It To Work

"No way should we share the credit," said Laura.

Laura, Ted and Shane were members of the same creative concept team at the largest advertising agency in the city. Their team, as well as another team consisting of three different agency employees received bonuses based on how much ad revenue they generated for the company each quarter.

Shane was pleased with the bonus his team had earned this quarter. It was the result of successfully pitching a new and creative idea for an ad campaign to a prospective client. The client loved the idea and as a result signed a lucrative three-year contract with the agency. The idea for the campaign had come from Shane but he knew it was the direct result of an informal conversation he had with a member of the agency's other ad team.

When he mentioned to his own team mates that he felt they should tell the boss that partial credit (and some of their bonus) should go to a member of the agency's other team, Ted agreed with Laura.

"No way should we give them partial credit", said Ted, "they wouldn't do it for us. And I don't know about you two, but I need all of this bonus just to catch up on my bills!"

What Do You Think?

Assume you were Shane and ask yourself these versions of the three key self-examination questions:

1. Would you care if Ted and Laura were told by your boss that you had informed her about the contribution from the other team member and that as a result their bonuses were reduced?

   _____

2. If you had contributed to the other team's success on a project, would you want that team to inform your boss about your effort? _____

3. How would you feel if members of your work team were never rewarded for assisting the efforts of others even if their contributions were significant? _____

   _____

Take It Away

"None of us are as valuable as all of us."

SECTION 3

Integrity in Internal Work Relationships

Topic 3: Ethical Situations Related to Employee Selection and Rewards

Consider This

In the popular sport of thoroughbred horse racing, some people think the fastest horse wins. In fact, that hasn't been true for nearly 150 years. That's because in 1860, Henry John Rous, a former British Admiral and steward at the English Jockey club introduced the weight-for-age (WFA) handicapping system still in use today.

WFA is a method of equalizing natural differences in race horses. For example, by the age of two, a horse has achieved 95% of its mature height and weight. By the end of its third year it is fully mature. If a two year old races a three year old, the more mature horse (because it is fully developed) would always win.

To make things equal in the race, the older horse is required to carry extra weight. The weights are made of lead and jockeys use saddle pads with pockets to hold the lead weights. In addition to age, allowances are made for other factors including the distance of the race and even the month in which the race is run.

Handicapping is common in many sports. But the paradoxical principle of handicapping; unbalancing the scales of equality to balance the scales of equality is always the same.

In the business world, employees cannot be handicapped based on some specified characteristics (such as race, religion, and gender for example). But that still doesn't mean selection; promotion and other job-related rewards always go to the most deserving candidates. And because of that, ethical issues can arise.

> *"Character cannot be developed in ease and quiet. Only through experience of trial and suffering can the soul be strengthened, ambition inspired, and success achieved."*
> *Helen Keller*

Put It To Work

"So you are recommending Ellie for the promotion?" asked Jeff, the Director of Human Resources for the Apex Company.

Jeff was talking to Rebecca, the manager of the company's customer service department. Rebecca had just informed Jeff she was leaning toward choosing Ellie rather than Marco to fill the vacancy created by the retirement of a supervisor who reported to Rebecca. The job meant a good raise for the staff member Rebecca chose to fill it.

"They both are certainly highly qualified," said Jeff, as he reviewed the two workers' performance records. Then he looked up from the files on his desk and asked, "What makes you think Ellie would be the better choice?"

"Well," replied Rebecca, "They are both really good, but I just found out that Ellie's husband lost his job. Marco's single. I think Ellie's family could use the extra money the raise would give them right now a lot more than Marco would."

What Do You Think?

Assume you were Rebecca and ask yourself these versions of the three key self-examination questions:

1. Would you care if Jeff told Marco the reason he did not get the promotion was because you felt Ellie's family needed the money more than he did? _____

2. Would you be willing to forgo your own promotion (or raise) if your boss felt the family situation of another worker in your department made that family more deserving of the reward than your own family? _____

3. Would you approve of an employee reward system in which all bosses were permitted to assess external factors (including family need) rather than worker merit when hiring, promoting or paying employees? _____

Take It Away

> *"Whether you choose to let your circumstances make you bitter or better, you'll be changed nonetheless."*

SECTION 3

Integrity in Internal Work Relationships

Topic 4: Ethical Situations Related to Restricted Information

Consider This

The purpose of restricting information is nearly always to protect a person or group from harm. Sometimes, keeping information secret can even be a matter of life or death. That was certainly the case in World War II when critical information needed to be passed among American military commanders in a way that could not be deciphered or decoded by the enemy.

The solution, in part, was provided by members of the Navajo Indian tribe. Over 400 Navajo Indians served as Marines in World War II. Their assignment was to pass coded messages important to winning that conflict.

Because they could talk in a language know only to them, it was impossible for the Germans, Italians or Japanese to decipher the messages even if they were intercepted. These Navajo "code talkers" were first deployed on Guadalcanal in 1942 and later served in Tinian, Guam, Iwo Jima, and Okinawa. Their messages were never successfully intercepted. On July 21, 2001 President Bush recognized their efforts and he awarded all of the code-talkers Congressional Gold Medals. Memorialized in John Woo's 2002 movie "Windtalkers," the Navajo's secret way of restricting information certainly helped the Allies while at the same time it frustrated their enemies.

The intent of restricting information is nearly always to help one person or group; but it can only do that by withholding the information from others. In business, the tricky part is often deciding just who should be helped and who should be kept uninformed. When you are the decider, ethical issues can easily arise!

> "To build an architecture of trust, it is better to be open than to seem open and it is better to be trustworthy than to seem trustworthy."
> Michael Tiemann

Put It To Work

"I really am looking forward to playing baseball for State College. I'm glad you recruited me," said Scott Joseph.

Scott was a star athletic at his high school and had been highly recruited nationally for his abilities on the baseball field. Scott was in his parents' living room talking to Coach Ron Paulson. Ron served as State College's assistant baseball coach.

"I narrowed my choices down to State College and one other school," continued Scott. "My parents could see me play more if I went to the other school, but they agreed I could learn a lot from Coach Saban. So we are going to accept the scholarship you have offered. We're going with State College because of Coach Saban."

Coach Saban was the Head Coach at State College and was indeed a rising star in the college baseball coaching ranks. As one of his assistants, however, Ron knew there would soon be an announcement that Coach Saban was leaving State College to accept a coaching job at a larger school. But that information was confidential and was not to be shared until the move was publicly announced.

What Do You Think?

Assume you were Coach Ron:

1. Would you care if Coach Saban found out that you had told Scott about his new coaching position? _____.
   Would you care if Scott's parents eventually found out you had know Coach Saban was leaving and that you did not share the information with them? _____

2. How would you feel if you accepted a new job position due primarily to the person you would be working for but found out after you had moved your family to the new area that the key person was leaving for a better job? _____.

3. Would you approve of a system in which each person in an organization got to decide what organizational information was to remain confidential and what information was to be made public? _____

Take It Away

"The promise not to reveal a secret is always superseded by your oath to be the person you were meant to be."

SECTION 3

Integrity in Internal Work Relationships

Topic 5: Ethical Situations Related to Compensation

Consider This

Looks can often be deceiving. That's certainly true with the ocean tides. If you are standing on a beach when the tide comes in, it may look like water is moving up the beach. Actually, the entire ocean is rising.

As the earth spins, the water on it is balanced evenly on all sides by centrifugal force. But the moon orbiting the earth places a gravitational pull on the water. This pull causes the water to bulge toward the moon.

The resulting areas of high water levels are high tides and the areas of low levels are low tides.

Since the earth and the moon rotate around the sun, it becomes an added factor. When the sun and moon are aligned, there are exceptionally strong gravitational forces, causing very high and very low tides.

As the earth, moon, and sun orbit the position of each one constantly changes. That causes slightly different gravitational effects. As a result, the water that looked like it was coming up the beach will actually rise and fall around the world at different times, at different rates and in different places.

In a similar way, when you first examine the cause of a business or organization's success, it can appear to be the result of the efforts of one person or small group. Upon closer inspection, however, the source of the success is more often than not the result of many worthy contributors; each of which is deserving of recognition and fair compensation.

> *"Don't worry when you are not recognized,*
> *but strive to be worthy of recognition."*
> *Abraham Lincoln*

Put It To Work

"So are we agreed that we recommend Tara for the job?" asked Allen.

Allen, Lara and Valerie served as a type of human resources sub-committee for the Steady Life Insurance Company. Their "hire" or "no hire" recommendation to the company president was almost always accepted.

The company had ten life insurance sales agents and now had one position vacancy. Each of the current agents made a salary of between $35,000 and $40,000 per year; with new agents generally making less and the more experienced agents earning more.

Tara had applied for the vacancy and was one of the best young sales agents Allen, Lara or Valerie had ever interviewed. Her references were exceptional and her work history indicated a real rising star. Allen and Lara wanted to offer the vacant position to Tara immediately. Valerie was not so sure.

"But she said she would only take the job if we offered her $75,000 per year," said Valerie.

"She makes $40,000 in her current job," replied Allen. "No way is she going to leave her current position without a significant increase. Anyway, the market for her kind of talent is always higher. I say we snap her up quick before our competition beats us to it."

What Do You Think?

Assume you were Valerie and ask yourself these versions of the three key self-examination questions:

1. Would you care if your company's currently employed agents were told you had recommended hiring Lara at the $75,000 salary level? _____

2. How would you react if you found your company had just hired someone to do a job identical to yours, but was paying that new person 50% more per year than you earned? _____

   _____

3. What do you think would happen in your company if all department heads were permitted to identify their "stars" and were allowed to pay them significantly higher wages than their peers? _____

Take It Away

> *"Justice is simply a commitment to give everyone what they are rightly owed."*

SECTION 4

Integrity in External Work Relationships

Topic 1: Ethical Situations Related to Customers

Consider This

Generally, sellers are free to establish their own prices for what they sell. But when buyers perceive prices to be too high, they are not usually shy about saying so, even when the price actually makes a good deal of sense.

Consider the price of popcorn in a movie theater. Nearly everyone (including you!) likely thinks the price is too high. When asked why popcorn costs so much most movie goers would reply it is because they are a captive audience. They think the owners can charge just about any price they want because you are not allowed to bring in your own popcorn.

Theater owners know better. The purpose of high popcorn prices is *not* to increase the money spent by each customer. That goal would be better achieved simply by selling popcorn for a bit less and raising ticket prices to cover the reduction. But then many attendees including large families, students, and those with lower incomes might not be able to attend the movies at a price they could afford! Charging a lot for popcorn helps keep ticket prices low.

Fair pricing, like many other customer oriented business issues, can be tricky and these type issues often lead to real ethical dilemmas!

> *"The way to gain a good reputation is to endeavor to be what you desire to appear.*
> Socrates

Put It To Work

Danielle had never seen such a snow storm. The snow had started Friday evening. By the time it stopped snowing on Saturday night the area had received nearly 18 inches of snow.

Now it was Sunday, one hour before opening. Danielle, the manager of the Buy Rite hardware store expected her store would be busy all day. As she thought about the various items customers would likely need because of the storm, Ralph, the store's assistant manger walked into her office.

"Danielle", said Ralph, "I just checked the inventory. We have 20 snow shovels left in stock. I wish we had 200. We would easily sell them all. The 20 shovels are currently priced at $19.99. I think we could raise the price to $39.99 and still sell all of them by noon. Shall I go ahead and mark them up?"

What Do You Think?

Assume you were Danielle and ask yourself these versions of the three key self-examination questions:

1. If you increased the price of shovels, would you care if the next day your local newspaper reported that you had done so? _____
   _____

2. How would you feel if you stopped at the local grocery store for milk on your way home from work and found that the store had doubled the price of milk because it also was in short supply due to the storm? _____

3. How do you think the general public in your area would view its local businesses if those businesses used the snow storm as a reason for increasing prices on items that were in high demand because of the storm? _____

Take It Away

"Where customers are put first, customers last."

SECTION 4

Integrity in External Work Relationships

Topic 2: Ethical Situations Related to Competitors

Consider This

Americans are fiercely competitive in sports and in business. This attitude was perhaps best captured by UCLA Bruins football coach "Red" Sanders who, in a 1955 Sports Illustrated article offered this famous quote: "*Sure, winning isn't every thing, It's the only thing.*" Others, however, including noted sports journalist Grantland Rice took a different approach in his equally famous statement that; *"it's not that you won or lost but how you played the game."*

In business, winning customers is most often the goal and the view that *"the ends justify the means"* is likely a familiar one to many who work in sales and marketing. In most cases, any legal action designed to gain customers is considered to be fair, it is expected and it is even admired. But not in all cases.

For example, in 2007 American toy makers recalled over ten million children's toys that had been manufactured with dangerous lead-based paint in foreign factories. As they recalled the toys, the toy makers expressed surprise and even innocence. After all, they stated, we were simply trying to give consumers the "low prices" they wanted most. And, they maintained, there is certainly nothing wrong with that.

But most people understand one more old American saying that: *"There's no free lunch"*. Cutting corners, reducing quality, and sacrificing fair work standards can indeed lead to lower prices and the winning of customers from competitors. But it can also lead to business decisions that harm those in society who most count on our business leaders to do the right thing.

"Win or lose, do it fairly.
Knute Rockne

Put It To Work

"I'm pretty busy here, what's the problem?" asked Jacob Marley.

"Well, it's the bid submission checklist for the Retired Teacher's proposal," replied Joseph.

Joseph was a sales manager at the City Convention Center. Jacob was his boss. Joseph had been working hard to prepare a written bid to try and win the business of his city hosting the next annual meeting of the Association of Retired School Teachers. The group's yearly convention drew thousands of people to the city that hosted it, meant millions of dollars in revenue to local businesses and would be a real feather in the cap of any city that won the bid.

"What about it?" asked Jacob.

"It says in the bid request that cities that check this box on the application stating they are committed to environmentally friendly carbon footprint reduction practices will be given preference to win the bid," said Joseph.

"What do they mean by that?" asked Jacob.

"Well, they mean those organizations that are committed to practicing green conservation techniques. That's not really us. We don't employ green conservation methods. We don't even recycle the plastic water bottles from our meeting rooms," said Joseph.

"Joseph," said Jacob without looking up, "don't be a chump. You are not under oath. Just check the box. If they ask, we'll just tell them we are as *committed* to green practices as anyone else. And by green you and I both know it means the dollars this contract can bring in. Now I really need to get back to work. Do you have any other questions?"

What Do You Think?

Assume you were Joseph and ask yourself these versions of the three key self-examination questions:

1. If you checked the box, would you care if the bid reviewers had overheard your conversation with Jacob? _____

   _____

2. How would you feel if you lost a bid you had worked hard to assemble because another bidder was dishonest about an important aspect of the bid they had submitted? _____

   _____

3. What if all businesses took the position that any strategy designed to beat the competition that is not technically illegal must be permissible? _____

Take It Away

> *"It's nice to be good, but it's better to be good for something."*

SECTION 4

Integrity in External Work Relationships

Topic 3: Ethical Situations Related to Financial Reporting

Consider This

Every person knows that sometimes things are not really what they appear to be.

In fact, magicians make their living entertaining audiences by creating illusions of seemingly impossible or extraordinary feats using ordinary, but unseen and unknown techniques. In the U.S. perhaps the most famous illusionist of all time was Ehrich Weiss.

You may not know him as Ehrich Weiss because Ehrich would ultimately adopt his stage name from a famous French magician whose birth name was Jean Eugène Robert.

Born in 1805, Jean Eugène Robert is considered by most magicians to be father of modern illusionism. In 1830, Jean Eugène married Josèphe Cecile Houdin and shortly thereafter, under special dispensation from the French government, was allowed to use the hyphenated last name of Jean Eugène Robert-Houdin.

Adding an "I" to the name Houdin, Hungarian born Ehrich Weiss would, fifty years later, ultimately perform across the entire world as *Harry Houdini*; an illusionist who, in keeping with his craft, even adopted a stage name that was more illusion than reality.

Perhaps no area of business is more subject to the craft of an illusionist than financial reporting. Because that is true, the ethical issues related to transparency in financial reporting are as important as they are ongoing.

"That you may maintain your self-respect, it is better to displease people by doing what you know is right, than to temporarily please them by doing what you know is wrong."
William J. Boetcker

Put It To Work

It was a Saturday afternoon and the two friends on the outdoor patio had just finished eighteen holes of golf. Pat was the chief financial officer (CFO) and Shingi was the human resources director at Norne Industries. As they sipped their drinks, Pat said, "I don't know if I should tell you this, but are you aware of what Dante is doing?"

Dante Laddon served as VP of Sales at Norne. He had been hired two years ago by Jim Starks, his college roommate and for the past five years the CEO of Norne Industries. As the CEO, Jim reported directly to Peggy Richards, the 64 year old founder of the company and now the Chairman of the Board.

"No. What's he doing?" asked Shingi.

"Well, he has been asking my people to increase the company's sales forecasts based on some pretty aggressive and I think pretty far out revenue assumptions. In my opinion, the forecasts come close to outright scamming the numbers. It makes our sales growth projections, and Dante's team look good, but I'm worried that if Jim or Peggy really understood how flimsy these forecasts are, maybe they would do things differently. As it is, if these sales don't materialize, and I can't see how they could, our company credibility for accurate revenue forecasting is going to go down the drain. Along with the wealth of anybody who bought our stock based on these shaky sales forecasts. I wonder if I should say anything to Jim?" said Pat.

"I wonder if Jim already knows," said Shingi.

What Do You Think?

Assume you were Shingi and you were concerned about ethical financial reporting in your company. Ask yourself these versions of the three key self-examination questions:

1. If you decided to bring your concern about Dante to Jim or Peggy Richards, would you care if Peggy told them about your concern? _____. Would you care if Peggy told them that it was Pat who had first shared the issue with you? _____

2. Would you care if, without first talking to you, Dante went directly to Jim or Peggy with a concern he had about how you operate your own department? _____

3. As a member of senior management, does Pat have a duty to the company's stockholders, employees and customers to report potential irregularities in financial reporting? _____ Do you have the same duty? _____

Take It Away

> *"Padding your expense account too much can turn it into severance pay."*

SECTION 4

Integrity in External Work Relationships

Topic 4: Ethical Situations Related to Societal Harm

Consider This

Not many people know that William Morrison of Des Moines, Iowa developed a car capable of running for 13 consecutive hours on one battery charge. Interestingly, he did so in 1890.

Unfortunately for Bill, the cost of gasoline was so low the car created little interest. Americans picked the lower cost option. Given all we now know about petroleum-based energy reserves, the possibility of increased environmental damage and the global impact of expanding energy consumption, Americans today face the same questions as those in 1890. Increasingly, however, the greater question may be; *how long can we, and our world, afford to pick our lowest cost option?*

What we know better now than we did in 1890, is that no person lives in isolation. Because we are part of a greater societal setting, when we think of what's best for us, it really means we must first define **us** as our families, our neighbors, our communities, our country, our planet and even our universe.

In so many of the ethical choices we encounter, the closer you look, the bigger becomes the impact of those choices. And the impact is not just on the **us** of today, but also on the **us** of the future. The actions we think are right or wrong now can only come into clear focus when viewed through the prism of tomorrow.

> *"Our most basic common link is that we all inhabit this small planet. We all breathe the same air. We all cherish our children's future. And we are all mortal."*
> *John F. Kennedy*

Put It To Work

Cynthia Larson is a buyer employed at Jefferson Mutual insurance company's home office in Pittsfield. In her role, she purchases office furniture for the company. Lamont Davis owns Pittsfield Furnishings, a mid-sized and high quality office furniture company.

Recently, Cynthia informed Lamont that she had decided to place the order to buy all new furnishings needed to complete Jefferson's large facility expansion from a supplier located in a different country. When

Lamont asked why, Cynthia replied that the foreign supplier could provide the needed furnishings for 5% less than the bid submitted by Pittsfield Furnishings.

Pittsfield Furnishings is one of the larger employers in town and each year has contributed significant financial resources to social services and charity fund-raising efforts in the local community.

What Do You Think?

Assume you were Cynthia and ask these versions of the three self-examination questions

1. Could you defend?
Your action to your boss? _____
Your action to your community leaders? _____

2. Would you care?
If one of Jefferson's best customers made a similar decision about buying from a different company? _____

3. What if everyone?
Chose the lowest cost product or service provider regardless of that organization's contribution to their local community?

_____

Take It Away

"We risk losing a fragment of our own humanity each time we act without respect to human consequences.

SECTION 4

Integrity in External Work Relationships

Topic 5: Ethical Situations Related to an Unethical Workplace

Consider This

A lot of people think Andrew Zimmern is a bit crazy. Zimmern is a food writer, TV personality, chef, teacher and is regarded as one of the most versatile and knowledgeable personalities in the food world.

As the co-creator, host and contributing producer of Travel Channel's hit series, Bizarre Foods with Andrew Zimmern, he travels the world, exploring and tasting unusual foods. How unusual? In Morocco he sampled lamb's head and pigeon pie. In Spain he tried pig brains. In the Philippines he feasted on crickets and stuffed frogs. In Ecuador it was guinea pigs, piranhas, and live coconut grubs.

What makes Zimmern so successful is his willingness to accept without condemnation the very different food items that others value and enjoy.

In the business world, the fact that ethics are so personal can often mean that those who differ ethically from the norm (and thus certainly appear unethical) are often questioned and even condemned.

Those who enjoy the privilege of applying their own ethical values at work, however, must never lose sight of the fact that others have the same rights. This important concept was summarized beautifully by John F. Kennedy when he said; *"Tolerance implies no lack of commitment to one's own beliefs. Rather, it condemns the oppression and persecution of others' beliefs."*

> *"The test of courage comes when we are in the minority.*
> *The test of tolerance comes when we are in the majority."*
> *Ralph W. Sockman*

Put It To Work

"James, I'm stepping out of the office for a few hours. If my wife calls you, tell her I'm doing a late house showing and that I couldn't call her because I left my cell phone on my desk," said Dan.

James and Dan were both sales agents in the area's largest real estate company.

They had worked together for five years, were friends as well as colleagues and had often socialized with each other outside of work. Both were married and their wives were friends as well.

"I didn't know you had a showing scheduled," said James.

"James, be a friend. I didn't say I had a showing scheduled," replied Dan. "I said if my wife calls, tell her I'm at a showing."

What Do You Think?

Assume you were Dan and ask yourself these versions of the three key self-examination questions:

1. If you covered for Dan as he requested, would you care if the next day your wife found out about it? _____. Would you care of Dan's wife found out about it? _____

2. How would you feel if you found out that Dan's wife had helped mislead you about a questionable activity undertaken by your own wife? _____

3. If requested to do so, do you think individuals should support their friends in activities that they themselves find unethical but that their friends perhaps do not feel are wrong? _____

Take It Away

*"If you are going in the right direction,
all you have to do is keep going."*

SECTION 5

Measuring Ethical Success

Topic 1: Your Integrity: How Others View You

Consider This

While it is very true that how we are viewed by others matters to us, the reason why it matters is often misunderstood. Some people think that how others see us is significant because we care what they think. That's not often the case. What we really care about is what we think.

If you buy a new hat because you believe it makes you look good, you would likely be very pleased when others compliment your hat. But if they said the hat made you look ridiculous, you would not be so pleased. That's because their feedback was not consistent with how you perceived the hat, and yourself, when you bought it. But if you chose to wear a ridiculous hat to a funny costume party, any party attendees comments that your hat makes you look ridiculous are just fine! Their comments now fit perfectly with the image you sought to project.

It is important to us that the opinions of others mirror our own views. Because that is true, a negative perception about you, even from people you have not met before, and may never see again, can still be so troubling.

We care about other's views because we very much want them to see us as we see ourselves; wearing a lovely hat!

Failure to achieve the image you personally seek to project matters. Not because of what it makes others think of you, but because of what you think of you. That's why the self-examination questions posed in this book request you assess how your ethical decisions affect you personally. Where ethics are concerned, it's very personal. So it matters. Not because of what they think, but because of what YOU think!

> *"The greatest success in living lies not in never falling;*
> *but in rising every time we fall."*
> *Nelson Mandela*

Put It To Work

In the workplace, persons with a variety of backgrounds, morals and beliefs will undoubtedly encounter others with different ethical values. When that happens, some people may be openly critical of others. Perhaps that's inevitable. In fact, it's been said that the only way to avoid criticism is to do nothing and say nothing. But that's usually not possible at work!

When it is your own ethical decisions that are criticized, it can certainly be hurtful to you. But that's also why it is so important to carefully consider your own actions before you take them. That allows you to be firm in your ethical decisions despite the inevitable critics.

Always remember that criticism about you won't come from those self-satisfied folks who have no faults; it comes from those whose faults are merely different than your own!

It's simply not possible to please everyone. But the good news is you don't have to. You only have to please one. And you are that one.

What Do You Think?

1. Have you ever been unfairly criticized by someone for an ethical decision you made when you knew it was the right one for you to make? _____

2. Have you ever been critical of someone but then later discovered that your criticism of them was unfair? _____

3. Is it more important to you that you feel your own behavior is ethical or that you view the behavior of others as ethical? _____

    _____

Take It Away

> "While the gossipers are busy talking about you;
> they are, at least, letting some other poor soul rest!"

SECTION 5

Measuring Ethical Success

Topic 2: Your Integrity: How You View Yourself

Consider This

We care about how others view us because we care so deeply about how we see ourselves. How we see ourselves directly affects our contentment. Norman Vincent Peale understood that when he wrote his best selling book <u>The Power of Positive Thinking</u>. In that book, Peale proposed that the key to happiness is viewing your situation in life positively.

Further, he suggested that keeping a positive attitude would actually have the affect of improving a person's life.

Today, as researchers find out more and more about the workings of the human brain, it becomes increasingly clear that having a positive attitude is not just a state of mind; it is a state of body and soul as well. A positive attitude directly affects our health (by reducing anxiety, stress and stress-related heart disease), our finances (by allowing us to be more satisfied with what we have, rather than what we do not have), and even our personal relationships (because people respond more positively to positive people.)

Having a positive attitude is clearly good for you; but how do you get one? And how do you keep it? You begin by recognizing that when you have control over what you do in life, you have control over how you view your life.

When compromising your ethics leads to feelings of shame, guilt, or inadequacy it is nearly impossible to keep a positive attitude. When you make ethical decisions that lead to feelings of joy, pride, honor, generosity and compassion it's easy to feel good about yourself!

> *"Success is not the key to happiness. Happiness is the key to success."*
> *Albert Schweitzer*

Put It To Work

Because a person's profession is such a big part of their life, feeling successful at work is important.

To take real pleasure in your job you must maintain a positive attitude about the work you do, your co-workers and your employer. Sometimes it can be pretty hard to see how each of these factors encourages a positive mind-set. In fact, there may be times when they absolutely do not seem to help you stay positive!

At all times, however, you do have the ability to be confident about your own ethical behavior. As a result, positive feelings about *yourself* are directly under your control.

Putting your ethical values to work, while you are at work, lets you to take the first critical step toward viewing your job optimistically. That's because it is simply not possible to see the world of work positively unless you first see yourself positively.

When you seek success by making good ethical choices at work, the emphasis is on who you are, instead of the tasks you do or where you do them. Your positive attitude about yourself will become infectious. Just as a pebble thrown into the water causes a ripple effect that spreads outward in all directions, being confident in your own success will spread to others. That's the personal power you display to everyone when you choose ethical behavior.

What Do You Think?

1. How do you feel about yourself at work when you have done something you hope no one finds out about? _____

   _____

2. How do you feel about yourself when you make an ethical decision that makes you extremely proud? _____

   _____

3. Do you think it is the opinion of yourself or the opinion of others that most affects how you feel about your level of success in life? _____

Take It Away

"To find yourself successful, you must first find yourself."

Manufactured By: RR Donnelley
                    Momence, IL USA
                    January, 2011